Encore

ENCORE

A collection of new poems by Shin Dong-ok
Translated by Jeon Seung-hee

K POET

아시아

Contents

ENCORE

All Is Going Well

A child learning Chinese characters asks me what the character *min*, meaning people, represents. Searching in a dictionary, I discover its horrific origin: It supposedly imitates a slave on their knees having one eye stabbed with a needle-shaped torture instrument.

"You will be a restless wanderer on the earth," Cain washed his blood-smeared hands and looked up at the sky. He heard the earth cry, after drinking human blood for the first time.

The blood that wet the earth, as Cain washed his hands, was probably the same as the blood of the people. In the history created by someone or something, people are just those who exist in it.

Nevertheless, humans are suffering beings and thus are passionate beings because of that feeling of suffering.* Nevertheless, what matters to us is no other world than this world.**

Monthly gatherings for contemporary poetry were held at the Sajikdong Meeting Place. Memories of walking over the pedestrian overpass with my old mentor, under a spring sunset. Although it was a time when everything felt depressing and stifling,

In retrospect, it was a time that I felt all would be going well.

* A quote from Karl Marx, *Economic and Philosophic Manuscript of 1844.*
** A quote from Louis Althusser, *Philosophy and Marxism.*

In Sowol's Tune*

Like holding a few pomegranate seeds in its mouth, preserved in molasses throughout winter,

Again under a blooming black jetbead tree, behind the thickly layered white forsythia fence,

Shall I look at the flowers spreading in the shade of the fragrant snowbell and purple beautyberry? Even after wondering like that, would it come after spring flowers bloomed and withered here and there?

As if gently treading thin ice, helplessly melting and dissolving, over there, hastily flitting across a

Dahurian larch and camphor tree, a bird

* [Translator's Note] Sowol is the pen name of Kim Jeong-sik (1902-34), a writer famous for his contributions to early modern poetry through his poignant verses written in a style reminiscent of traditional Korean folk songs.

Encore

I hear that people bury the dead under the ground on that star,
That the dead sleeping in the depth of the ground, some day
Will be reborn as the smiles of their beloved

Around the tip of a budding withe
On a pussy willow, past the buds of camellia flowers,
The spring winds whirl, shuddering

Sorokdo Island

On a summer afternoon, rain streaked into an empty space set aside for weather in my diary, about ten entries of which I had written ahead of time, after my friend with a milky-white face, who had transferred to a school in Seoul, visited me, I sat under a wall like a shadow with lost steps. While sitting side by side, we were counting the sunrays splitting the sunset, spreading between clouds, the day was darkening span by span.

Meanwhile, on a day just ahead of my first sea—at dawn, I went to the *myeon* office by the first bus, and then, after transferring two more times through the Gwayeok Terminal, I got off a small liner. After passing by a schoolyard, where young mother and father were dumped side by side, on a dejected hill a little away, after passing by the Wall of Wailing, I turn a corner of the bell tower of the Sorok Catholic Church,

There at the Mongdol Beach I was with my two younger sisters and youngest brother, a toddler, green stones here and there, where chilly and damp winds blew through a big, dense Big Cone pine cluster, where nobody was around. Fine waves soaked my calves and disappeared over and over with touches that felt sharper, as they were unfamiliar to me under the "*shower from a few clouds*" amid surging waves that I had already drawn with crayons.

Smelling the Fragrance of White Lilies

It was when lilies were blooming on the green hills Smelling the fragrance of white lilies again,* I was fumbling down a rough and mottled road, like laddered hemp breeches

Last night, without fear, I passed by an unfamiliar and faraway land, unlit even by a single candle, simply relying on momentary light subsiding around my earflaps when my hair fluttered

Now, at dawn, where I seem to have arrived with difficulty, through all mornings and nights of the world, I gather my feet and lower my head toward the direction where tender light emerges sluggishly

The more my worn-out shoes get crumpled and worn down further, the more holes are born—holding my hands together with all my might, as I would to gather light with warmth collecting in every hole,

I ask back, while pressing down the road with my feet, wriggling and alive under them, whether I should rush further from here or stay with no end in sight—on a morning when a bird is flying upward from the toecaps of my shoes, which were crushed unawares.

* A phrase from a poem by Lee Eun-sang (1903-82), "Thinking of My Friend."

Lyricist

A house built with sparsely spaced bricks is stronger when it is collapsing The same is true of lyrics He composes them with the finest and tenderest breath in a marginal and forsaken style

Although he shares credit equally with others, in the name of the band, a bitter taste ascends to the tip of his tongue when they sing it together All solid metaphors have become rusty

“Although you cannot help us, we have to help you and guard your abodes within us until the end” — These are words of Etty Hillesum, written on the wall of Westerbork Concentration Camp*

Because he had to stop a woman from dying, from thrown stones, even at the moment when someone desperately called, he drew a few unknown letters in the sand That was all Jesus ever wrote

* [Translator's Note] Etty Hillesum was a young woman from Amsterdam who composed diaries for two years, before dying at Auschwitz in 1943.

The Personal History of the Phonograph

To complete an eternally continuing confession, we need to endure the infinite To complete the infinite, we needed the constraint of time Words of love amplified in the past tense, as shallow as an empty pocket

Although everyone knew the word that can stop time, once spoken, although we anxiously cried your name in our dreams, nobody could get up Words of love continued eternally creating waves

Future-addicts walked during the days before dawn, before night and day were divided—where were they heading? Some voices passed by the park, went over the hills, and subsided on the leaves of crepe myrtles near the bike path,

Edison invented a phonograph just because he wanted to keep and treasure the voices of his loved ones.

In the Lingering Effects of Realism

We wandered from stage to stage Whenever we stepped down from one, we changed our names and made up a different list Meanwhile, an icy dusty smell wafted from our shadows

At night when bare feet become larger than the bed, chords accompanied by bodily movements continued in our dreams Dreaming of a stage that would have been impossible whenever other than in that moment

The scale was complete only when it commanded a few semitones Shoulder dances continue creakingly, and all gazes are pulled into the scale while whirling around

Although each wandered to look for different rhythms, pupils were two repeat signs facing each other Songs we exchanged were like a maze.

Doesn't it seem that the lingering effects of realism are wafting from somewhere? As if to say that there is no refrain that anyone can sing along with, there's a small hole in the corner of a rusty mirror ball

Until the moment when we fall asleep in the rainbow light pouring down, while being finely split, fingering and fingering Reality appropriate for improvisations remain Love good for variations overflows

Copy and Featuring

In June a stage was set up over the pile of basalt rocks on a beach, and someone spread one of their fingers and drew a circle in the air: *one, two, three, four*

We protested that we continued the riff, as something made us continue to play, as something made us continue to live the stage

That we had only continued to live, that, after embellishing all those codas and da capo al codas over and over, until they reached the state where there was no room for further embellishment, and then after putting in a lengthy comma,

We had run until the area around our lives would be completely dissolved in a brilliant light *What distinguishes copying and patronage is name value, so make a name!*

The promoter said that a perfect name is like an impulse or rhythm, that it will expand its map to the area where it will someday exceed its life

Into the thick southern forest, the sound of a nameless band penetrated Beyond the wet fog where a nameless concert that could not shake even a single leaf was dissolved

A group of drunkards drew near and soon noisy conversations surrounded the band Because the music was too quiet, even whispering conversations sounded like passionate confessions As the music was so quiet

Snow Effect

Leading children like snowflakes and women like snowstorms, he headed to an unfamiliar village near Paris On the first day, after demolishing the barn walls, he put the snow-covered mountain in the window Although he had been driven out, houses under the snow-covered roofs beyond the easel were just white houses covered with snow Under the eaves, connected like natural-dyed quilts, donkeys, rabbits, and children must be sleeping They must be sleeping mixed with cozy heaps of straws in the night of snowstorms

That blue is the sky, but, once hidden behind a palm, it does not shine any more

In the city, there is a sound of wheels and chains turning under the roofs

During that time, human beings fought with steam and painters often painted roofs

He titled it *A Road to Vetheuil or Snow Effect.* After signing it, he cut and kept it in his chest A snowstorm followed him from Argenteuil to Vetheuil and was about to blow from Vetheuil to Giverny Even on the lotus petals, leaves, and stamens, snowflakes occasionally fluttered and landed Since that day, snowstorms had never stopped behind Monet's back Flying upward from among the snowflakes, a bird

Life on the Score

In each word there is length, a high and low, and also breaths In every numbered book, sentences with different expressions and destined to have different fates

Delicately continued and then discontinued somewhere Inside the Babel Tower full of all kinds of lyrics written by poets gathered from all directions, like patchwork wrapping-cloth pieced together with exclamations and sighs

As it seemed I would meet the true owner of the scale someday, if I continued to count numbers inscribed in my forehead and heart, the setlist was meaningless any longer,

The reverberations of the coda that had bitten off, in a single bite, even the darkness spreading to the pupils, after covering the land on which we stood in the cozy feeling of the trifling comfort that we shared a single language

Improvisation continuing in the belief that it would someday continue into a better wave A single night formed through it A single *progressive* Perhaps the last *progressive* that we exchanged with life itself

Strum

Harmony is magic that calms silence with the speeding up of understanding

While building a road, harmony changes it

To flick six strings at the same time

Is to open a new era, to create a new world

Things Buried in Side B

You must think that, if you return after a long time away, you'd be embraced so tightly as to be stifled and your chest to be crushed Someone must be standing against the windowsill to do that

Someone is bound to come near the windowsill And then that someone will be affixed there, waiting for someone else to return Dead leaves might accumulate on the windowsill

And someone might paste music paper to the window, as a music stand, play music expectantly, and then fall asleep Dead leaves might accumulate layer by layer in the soundbox of the finger holes

And someday they might scream so loudly that the sound will sweep away the entire neighborhood that the darned fucker would disappear forever, that all would end up disappearing Even after everything disappeared like that,

If there was someone who found a riff to be properly walked, and then was enraptured with a scale in its center, while enduring curses and condemnations, being inscribed in the skin as by a heated iron

The vinyl they inscribed after cutting over and

over is 7 inches long It is easy for them to hide, but it won't be easy to reappear

Side A chosen after careful consideration is composed of only 2 tracks If everyone points fingers, saying we were wrong, then, although it might feel like beating someone to death or burying someone alive, we are just a band

Let's say it's okay to live the life of chores: keeping house, shopping for groceries, doing dishes, by piecing together a scale, after accidentally entering this world, who on earth is the leader?

Botanist

He lived while being buried in pots As he was a picky eater, he managed to feed himself only with insects and leaves While alive, he was treated as a madman Nobody accepted his opinions It took a hundred years for his journals to be read again

A hundred years was enough time to put a person's madness to sleep

It was a time when the world was not like in these days The past was peaceful inside a latched closet, nobody looked absurdly faraway, and nobody walked backward

Holding a magnifying glass in his hand within the time that was now, which had become old, as it was both faraway and nearby

On a Tour Bus

Snowstorm and torrential rain can appear without notice and may pour all night long Like waterdrops that were nothing and on the side of no one, and came from nobody knows where

Songs have no more place to penetrate, but fans overflow wherever they go and tours continue There is a world even in a single waterdrop dripping askew on a bus window, and this world is full of groupies worshipping only themselves

The man's age has no importance He could be very old or very young What's important is that he does not know where he is, and that he wants to go somewhere*

* A quote from Louis Althusser, *Portrait of a Materialist Philosopher.*

Rhapsody

They made a song stop over a song, and created a wall with winds Built a well by collecting clouds Engraved bees and butterflies on the windowsill There were portraits, the histories of which could not be presumed in every four-way layout wriggling and stretching outward

As they seemed to pull up the boots to the navel, after getting up from a chair mended with a finely tanned leather patch, suddenly a crossbeam was hung in the air They blew breaths containing the same reverberations into the rooftiles and the gate

There were winds, full of fibrous roots, leaving

the yard after making a round, and young sprouts spreading their veins in the direction where sunset was also spreading, and a troll made of cool murmurings just drawn from a remote forest

When they sat at the table, as if bowing after taking off last season's coat and shaking disheveled hair, the life of silence standing tall, after turning away from housekeeping built with effort, was a dead-end wall like that

Wanting not to leave an empty space, he tied up sceneries to the song Although his heart is ripening yellow next to the fireplace, where the fire is crunching under the valley wind, following only remote paths where darkness falls first

Let's sing that the night is not yet deep Let's sing that the night is not yet deep and then let's stop a song over a song and let's muster courage A singer originally means a person who sews, a person who sews and raises

We are either in this song or that song As there is no exit from this world, there is no exit from a song There is no other side

Tribute Day

The last was always a tribute song That was an unwritten law of a scene Because a person who had to leave at some point would not leave dust on or touch someone else's instrument, breaths were trembling in the crevice of the hinges of a door closing with a creaking sound

While containing expressions of all the people coming in and out of the open door like that, harmony stretched out How strange that it is to be anything at all! Secrets are sleeping in winter clothes*

What is your gesture when you're in despair?

Dancing is that kind of a question Over the tearful retina, a wall recedes while approaching Rhythm is that kind of pressure

We walked side by side with the moon We had breakfast together and, after sharing the sunset, we found and sat on a still warm spot under the wall When the moon was rising over the corner of the stage half torn down

While drinking wine from a kettle heated black in the dark orange moonlight brightening here and there in the black-blue darkness, like an Asian tiger snake, we asked, *Is this really the revolution we achieved?*

Although they say we wrote a new revolution, while wailing against a wall in an underground garage, in an abandoned factory, creating a genre off chart and outside of a stage, where in the world is a revolution that is not happy even as much as a fingernail?

Like greetings that disappeared into the past but are flying to us from the future, songs continue and that was the life of a band Writing new songs while wandering around the streets after cramming instruments and speakers into a trunk

Therefore, isn't the fact that we have become anything at all mysterious enough? Revolution is dirty and secrets sleep in winter clothes

* From Neutral Milk Hotel's "In the Aeroplane Over the Sea." Its lyrics include "All secrets sleep in winter clothes....Can't believe how strange it is to be anything at all."

Songs Requested at Noon

Without understanding the sound of birds calling, without quoting the whisperings of dead souls, but growing nettles and plantains at its sides unawares

At a time when I was tuning the instrument called the earth, a time when I was trying to quiet the feeling that there remained only a worn-out record, in the waves of concentric circles into which a bell sound died down

When, remembering the days when songs of love were reverberating if I bought tangible music and turned up the volume, I spread and read the insert, shy words of confession reaching my ears

Song of Songs

Over there beyond there
In endless refrains, in the strike of a sound wave
While purifying dreams of the dead and opening toward another conclusion
Collecting and embracing all affectionate auricles of the world
Endlessly approaching as a barricade, as an ark
Sharing this moment endlessly carnifying
This song whirling like rough waters in the pulse
Is an enormous promise
Changing all human beings

Page-Turner

In the fall of that year, the first snow came Leaving behind hesitant friends holding desperately onto a windowsill, and exchanging words of love that would quickly evaporate or be forgotten

Holding a tiny light in their arms, people continuously entering the concert hall through the snowstorm Their ankles stepping down to the snow-covered road were as white as a flute

In that love there was music As the love of God should eternally continue even if God dies, there was music in that love with the stubborn form of freedom

Beating scores transformed lives every time
Successful concerts left burdensome name value
and at their end the human was no longer human

When music ends, humans are mere dust

POET'S NOTE

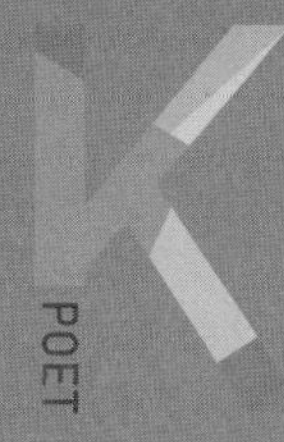

I heard that a guitarist died of a heart attack while on a vacation with his grandson on a beach in Mexico. Listening to "Entre dos Aguas," I feel like I can still hear his heartbeat. Another guitarist died cradling his guitar in his arms in an apartment in Oslo, Norway. He played in a band, Madrugada, which is a Spanish word meaning "dawn." It rained over his memorial concert, which began with a bird flying by and drawing a line in a dry winter sky.

Yet another guitarist was born in a countryside. His father was an active soldier, so he grew up with his grandparents and an elder sister. A guitar he received for his birthday and blues music nurtured him. As a young man, he achieved everything that a music with an electric guitar can achieve. He lost loved ones and indulged in an impossible love affair. Succumbed to alcohol and drugs, he cursed people he had once loved. He lost a child to an accident. The moment he shone brightest in music was his youthful days. Yet most people seemed to love him performing again after he had lost everything. This is the story Eric Clapton wrote in *Life in 12 Bars,* yet it could also encompass the story of an ordinary, warm-hearted neighbor.

Some deaths exist always beyond sentences, but they stay near our lives to the last. Once I wrote poems mourning the deaths of my teachers, family, and friends, gradually risking tearing down my life. However, I can neither understand the sounds of birds nor quote the whispering voices of the dead with my sentences. A long silence always continues. The time and space emerging from that silence have you and me facing each other. I remember the moments I bought tangible music, while measuring that distance, and reading inserts, as if spreading a letter from a tender lover: Things happening when great love songs reverberated, as I turned up the volume.

I once drew a house with breakably brilliant windows. It was too perfect for me to build on this earth, where I stand. I learned that since the house I drew cannot collapse, it cannot exist in real life. I also learned that I don't have to draw a faraway place just because I dream of warm light. There will always remain light somewhere that cannot recede, no matter how much one tries to hide it. This book began with my intention to relive those moments when light remained in the midst of your and my lives.

As they are faraway, and yet nearby, I remember

those with whom I shared life during the worn-out present. Most of the time we shared continues eternally in the present tense. Precious moments will be peaceful behind bolted doors. As nobody walks backward, we were together in the time running to eternity. We'll always be together.

POET'S ESSAY

Meta-Life

During the kite-flying season, I wandered around bamboo forests behind my house. Nobody scolded me for cutting and taking dead bamboo. By pulling at bamboo parts, while holding a sickle upside-down and securing its handle between my feet, I stripped away soft flesh inside bamboo trees and left the smooth outside hull as much as possible. Around the time the new year approached, I found old calendars were useful for my kite-making. If I didn't have old calendars, the smooth part of the inside of a fodder bag, made of layers of paper, was good, too. While all my family was sleeping, I would sit on the wooden floor of the storeroom and make a kite. After bending and pasting the ribs onto a piece of paper, I leveled and finished it by pasting on tails. Then, if I found it was still uneven, I would balance it by adding small pieces of paper. Then I collected bundles of string and wound them around a bobbin.

Behind a bamboo forest, there were a barley field and a peony field. When barley sprouted and when it became dark green, it was okay to tread on. When the kite revealed its face, fully embracing winds, after bending softly, I lay on the barley field and read books like *Treasure Island* and *Two Years' Vacation,* after sticking the bobbin with thread into a furrow. I fell asleep, unawares that ice was forming under my back. I starched the kite string, mixing the starch with finely ground glass. I learned the meaning of the phrase "the edge is blue," that it means the edge is so sharp that it looks blue. The starched string drew rays of light both tender and sharp. The afterglow stretching below the moonlight continued faraway into the night sky. When I grabbed the bobbin tightly and cut the string, a fish leisurely disappeared while swinging its fin into the other side of the sky surrounded by blue moonlight. After embroidering an unknown pattern around the sky, it left a dark blue spot.

*

I can still feel vividly how my hands felt the moment I grasped the handle of the bobbin more forcefully, after cutting the string. I remember a certain power that engulfed my entire body from my fingertips to my toes and then quickly slipped away the moment I let go of the kite. I clearly remember that certain and substantial power that captures our lives only at the moment we let it go. I remember the sense of being connected with something in my entire body only at the moment when I cut off a taut string with my own hands, a string so taut it would not allow different thought to interfere with it. The joy of disappearance. Perhaps sentences continue to fully forget. It was Charles Sanders Peirce who said, "Let us not pretend to doubt in philosophy what we do not doubt in our hearts." Let us not pretend to doubt in poetry what we do not doubt in our hearts. The dilemma between experience-based inductive reasoning and imagination is not a matter of value. They belong to different dimensions. It was David Hume who said something to the effect that human beings can repeatedly transition to an apparently trivial but more important dimension through the delicacy that is at the heart of our everyday lives.

*

Sometimes, I dream of becoming a bird and flying off in the sky. Although I don't know whether I am the bird, or the bird is me in this dream, I leisurely drift around in the sky, enjoying a bird's-eye view and making contact with time and space. Looking down from the sky, my neighborhood is like a small bead. Faraway, the same dots move sluggishly in a direction. When I approach them, and wave my hand, they are all warm faces. Going out of the back gate of the elementary school in front of my house, I pass by the subway station, ride a rocking car on the rooftop of a department store, and endlessly fly along the Naebu-sunhwan-ro Road behind the dreamy forest of northern Seoul. When I spread what might be either a wing or a hand, someone beside me always catches it with their hands. Warm and tiny hands. It might have been my late grandfather who said that a pitchfork is stuck even in water in a small soy-sauce bowl. Although both water and a mirror eat light, there is always a center that light touches first even in a smoothly rubbed mirror. Right there, lips through which the mirror says something to a human being are slowly moving. The sound of the light is usually plosive. They submerge in water and then in light. What floats up after being submerged is not the trace of someone who traversed into the light, into the water forever; what floats up is rather the trace of a memory that the absence of all people, no matter who, sank deeply into the water.

*

Once, I used sentences, the expression on whose faces became livelier when they lied. Or I could call it imagination or delusion rather than lies. If I called them dreams, I could have them address the life of a person, whoever they are. In other words, I used to write poems that said, expressed, thought, and felt nothing. That might have been possible because I was good at taking my poems to a place where no one could look in, a place deep in my heart that nobody knew. While *meta-language* must be based on doubts about existence, if there is such a thing as the other side of *meta*, there might be a way of writing poems that can be *structurally* verified in all languages. Also, creation outside of interpretation and intentions may be possible at the moment when we reject meta-language. Perhaps we can say that the moment when the quality of *meta* disappears is the starting point of an event where desire and the unconscious transform? Logically, that would be the case. Yet, if that's the case, the place for imitation, otherness, and the language of appropriation, empathizing in each person every moment when we are vividly and independently alive and wriggling, disappears. That's because everyday language that makes it possible for poetry to continue would become useless. As we have passed through the time when magical imitation of the other transforms into violence, rejecting the quality of *meta* might have been able to lead to a correct conclusion. Therefore, we may declare and accept rightly in many ways that meta-language does not exist.

*

My sentences always stand a little aside: the axes

that I build while continuing to stand aside every step of the way. Language, position, perspective that stand aside, even while standing next to one another, create trivial yet important deviations. The small delicacy that creates those small deviations blends existence, dreams, and reality. I think that such might have been the case so far.

COMMENTARY

Songs That Will Not End

Cho Daehan (Literary Critic)

It is widely known that Orpheus' elegy, which reverberated in hearts across the Lethe, was played on a lyre, and that the name of that instrument and "lyric" share an etymology. However, it is less known that his songs were a sort of mnemonic device. At that time, the gods, who had won the Giganto Maxia War against the giants, wanted to record the story of their lengthy conflict, but they didn't know how best to do it. Thus, they tried to write a song together with the goddess of memory, Mnemosyne, to commemorate and celebrate it. As a result, the nine muses, including Kaliope, were born, and the poet and musician Orpheus was their descendant. In other words, poems and songs were products of a will to make sure to remember, like the efforts of the scientist-inventor, who created a phonograph "because he wanted to keep and treasure the voices of his loved ones" ("The Personal History of the Phonograph").

Encore by Shin Dong-ok also feels like his record and song lyric of a time that he loved and fought for. It contains "shy words of confession reaching [his] ears," when "[he] spreads and reads the insert" and the memories of "days when songs of love were reverberating if I bought tangible music and turned up the volume ("Songs Requested at Noon")." They could also be the "words of love" and the music "in that love" that a poet, who seems to believe that "the love of God should eternally continue even if God dies," insisted on recording ("Page-Turner").

The botanist, whom the poet describes as being "treated as a madman" while alive, might have been quite happy until he died ("Botanist"). Although he spent his entire life buried in leaves and pots, he must have had dreams for an unknown future and pride in singing a secret song that no one in the world could have understood. During that time, when he was truthful to his own time, "[t]he past was peaceful inside a latched closet, nobody looked absurdly faraway, and nobody walked backward ("Botanist")." However, what other meaning than the joy of consuming familiar melodies like memories would singing the song of past enthusiasm and future dreams have here, where all passions and political dreams for revolution are sleeping in our unconscious, and during the coda of a song that already reached the climax?

The psychoanalyst, author, and English professor

Molly A. Rothenberg understand us living in this world as beings to be perfected in the future. According to her, we are beings open to the future, who borrow parts of our beings from the future. By this, Rothenberg does not simply acknowledge the infinite possibilities of the future, but emphasizes the uncertainty of the beings in the present, which will turn out to be the past in the future. That is, the meanings of utterances and actions of the beings in the present can be determined only after the future brings interpretation and intervention. As the life of a madman, who was merely a single being, was finally rearranged as the meaningful life of a botanist only after future discoveries and re-evaluation, repetition and interpretation in the future-perfect are necessary to understand the "empty" meaning of an action. "It took a hundred years" for the journals of the botanist, whose opinion "nobody accepted" then, to be read again ("Botanist"). Thus, wouldn't we need more time and reenactment than 100 years for the song lyrics of dreams, love, and revolution to recover their true meanings?

Hence, Shin Dong-ok's *Encore* is not a simple elegy of older days, but dreams of the past yet to be perfected and the lyrics of a song yet to be finished. "Like greetings that disappeared into the past, but are flying to us from the future, songs continue ("Tribute Day"), and repeat while looking at each other's pupils, like "two repeat-signs facing each other ("In the Lingering Effects of Realism")." On an empty stage, where nobody requests an encore, the poet recites "a troll made of cool murmurings just drawn from a remote forest" again, after "taking off last season's coat and shaking disheveled hair" and "bowing [to the audience] ("Rhapsody")."

I hear that people bury the dead under the ground on that star,
That the dead sleeping in the depth of the ground, some day
Will be reborn as the smiles of their beloved

—"Encore" (excerpt)

Let's return to the afore-mentioned "old story" again. As is well known, the attempt of Orpheus to cross the Lethe, one of the five rivers of the underworld, called the river of unmindfulness, to take back his lover failed because of his foolish action of looking back, against a caution not to do so. However, after his forgetting, it might have been natural for him as a poet to choose a life captivated by the memories of the past, rather than living a life in a new world. A poet, even then, meant a person who understood that "[a]s there is no exit from this world, there is no exit from a song ("Rhapsody"), and, thus, insisted on remaining in it and repeating the songs of old memories. He remains the only scribe of memories, who was not swept by the river of forgetting after drinking the spring water of Mnemosyne. Wouldn't the only way to revive "the dead sleeping in the depth of the ground" in this trivial star, where all secrets of the other side are exhausted and no miracle happens, be remembering and singing about someone? The poets' performance seems to begin again through the prayer that someday that old dream "[w]ill be reborn as the smiles of their beloved" and "in the belief that it would someday continue into a better wave ("Life on the Score")."

The old rhapsody they sang is known to be a word that unites *rhaptein*, meaning "to sew," and *oidia,* meaning a "song." Shin Dong-ok, too, seems to piece together dreams and beautiful memories of the past, discordant with the foundation of the present time, "like natural-dyed quilts ("Snow Effect")." Like the botanist 100 years ago, would the future when their songs will be surrounded by bright curtain call come? It would be in vain to be sure, but the poet's songs might be "the last *progressive* that we exchanged with life itself ("Life on the Score")" and remains with us. For the person who still believes that the power of the song lyric—composed "with the finest and tenderest breath in a marginal and forsaken style ("Lyricist")" for that dreamlike moment when "[t]his song whirling like rough waters in the pulse"—is "[c]hanging all human beings ("Song of Songs"), it seems that the poet's never-ending song will continue.

WHAT THEY SAY ABOUT SHIN DONG-OK

K

POET

We cannot ask for a total structure of our poetry from a single poet. Yet in the career of poet Shin Dong-ok we find two wills that have formed the foundation of our poetry since the 2000s: the will to become the king of a system and the will to become the system of a king. As the former, poetry contains conclusiveness, because a significance map leading to the kingdom of ethics is embedded in it. As the latter, poetry serves the power of utterance.... At least Shin Dong-ok seems to maintain this center. It is because of this career, examined above, that I expect from this poet, standing in the center, continuing to circle and split, that he become a new foundation, instead of repeating the 21st century so far, in which meanings and reverberations have opposed each other.

Cho Kang Sok (literary critic), "Judge' s Remark,"

Sseulm 11 (2020 Fall–Winter)

His poems have sometimes combined with political thought, vigorously testifying to the terrifying violence of reality, and, at other times, have openly desired the passionate unfolding of themselves. To him, poetry has developed and worked as a linguistic construct that forcefully conveys many thoughts and premonitions. Thus, his poems have been written in the dimension of aesthetics and thought, rather than rhetoric and description. As a result, poetry has been a sort of language inherent in existence that forms aesthetic crystals, rather than as a language of simple description. I hope that his poems, which have conducted what Francois Raymond called a "sudden invasion of mysteriousness into everyday lives," while fundamentally fracturing ancient principle of lyricism, would ascend as an alternative method, helping our poetry, characterized as it is by the absence of metaphysical trembling, by overcoming its poverty and lightness.

Yoo Sung Ho (literary critic), "Delicately Shining, White and Beautiful Steps," *The Night Will Continue* (Seoul, Minumsa, 2019)

K-POET
Encore

Written by Shin Dong-ok
Translated by Jeon Seung-hee
Published by ASIA Publishers
Address 445, Hoedong-gil, Paju-si, Gyeonggi-do, Korea
Tel (8231).944.5058
Email bookasia@hanmail.net
Homepage Address www.bookasia.org

ISBN 979-11-5662-317-5 (set) | 979-11-5662-620-6 (04810)
First published in Korea by ASIA Publishers 2022

This book is published with the support of the Literature Translation Institute of Korea (LTI Korea).

바이링궐 에디션 한국 대표 소설

한국문학의 가장 중요하고 첨예한 문제의식을 가진 작가들의 대표작을 주제별로 선정!
하버드 한국학 연구원 및 세계 각국의 한국문학 전문 번역진이 참여한 번역 시리즈!
미국 하버드대학교와 컬럼비아대학교 동아시아학과, 캐나다 브리티시컬럼비아대학교 아시아학과 등 해외 대학에서 교재로 채택!

바이링궐 에디션 한국 대표 소설 set 1

분단 Division

01 병신과 머저리-**이청준** The Wounded-**Yi Cheong-jun**
02 어둠의 혼-**김원일** Soul of Darkness-**Kim Won-il**
03 순이삼촌-**현기영** Sun-i Samch'on-**Hyun Ki-young**
04 엄마의 말뚝 1-**박완서** Mother's Stake I-**Park Wan-suh**
05 유형의 땅-**조정래** The Land of the Banished-**Jo Jung-rae**

산업화 Industrialization

06 무진기행-**김승옥** Record of a Journey to Mujin-**Kim Seung-ok**
07 삼포 가는 길-**황석영** The Road to Sampo-**Hwang Sok-yong**
08 아홉 켤레의 구두로 남은 사내-**윤흥길** The Man Who Was Left as Nine Pairs of Shoes-**Yun Heung-gil**
09 돌아온 우리의 친구-**신상웅** Our Friend's Homecoming-**Shin Sang-ung**
10 원미동 시인-**양귀자** The Poet of Wŏnmi-dong-**Yang Kwi-ja**

여성 Women

11 중국인 거리-**오정희** Chinatown-**Oh Jung-hee**
12 풍금이 있던 자리-**신경숙** The Place Where the Harmonium Was-**Shin Kyung-sook**
13 하나코는 없다-**최윤** The Last of Hanak'o-**Ch'oe Yun**
14 인간에 대한 예의-**공지영** Human Decency-**Gong Ji-young**
15 빈처-**은희경** Poor Man's Wife-**Eun Hee-kyung**

바이링궐 에디션 한국 대표 소설 set 2

자유 Liberty

16 필론의 돼지-**이문열** Pilon's Pig-**Yi Mun-yol**
17 슬로우 불릿-**이대환** Slow Bullet-**Lee Dae-hwan**
18 직선과 독가스-**임철우** Straight Lines and Poison Gas-**Lim Chul-woo**
19 깃발-**홍희담** The Flag-**Hong Hee-dam**
20 새벽 출정-**방현석** Off to Battle at Dawn-**Bang Hyeon-seok**

사랑과 연애 Love and Love Affairs

21 별을 사랑하는 마음으로-**윤후명** With the Love for the Stars-**Yun Hu-myong**
22 목련공원-**이승우** Magnolia Park-**Lee Seung-u**
23 칼에 찔린 자국-**김인숙** Stab-**Kim In-suk**
24 회복하는 인간-**한강** Convalescence-**Han Kang**
25 트렁크-**정이현** In the Trunk-**Jeong Yi-hyun**

남과 북 South and North

26 판문점-**이호철** Panmunjom-**Yi Ho-chol**
27 수난 이대-**하근찬** The Suffering of Two Generations-**Ha Geun-chan**
28 분지-**남정현** Land of Excrement-**Nam Jung-hyun**
29 봄 실상사-**정도상** Spring at Silsangsa Temple-**Jeong Do-sang**
30 은행나무 사랑-**김하기** Gingko Love-**Kim Ha-kee**

바이링궐 에디션 한국 대표 소설 set 3

서울 Seoul

31 눈사람 속의 검은 항아리-**김소진** The Dark Jar within the Snowman-**Kim So-jin**
32 오후, 가로지르다-**하성란** Traversing Afternoon-**Ha Seong-nan**
33 나는 봉천동에 산다-**조경란** I Live in Bongcheon-dong-**Jo Kyung-ran**
34 그렇습니까? 기린입니다-**박민규** Is That So? I'm A Giraffe-**Park Min-gyu**
35 성탄특선-**김애란** Christmas Specials-**Kim Ae-ran**

전통 Tradition

36 무자년의 가을 사흘-**서정인** Three Days of Autumn, 1948-**Su Jung-in**
37 유자소전-**이문구** A Brief Biography of Yuja-**Yi Mun-gu**
38 향기로운 우물 이야기-**박범신** The Fragrant Well-**Park Bum-shin**
39 월행-**송기원** A Journey under the Moonlight-**Song Ki-won**
40 협죽도 그늘 아래-**성석제** In the Shade of the Oleander-**Song Sok-ze**

아방가르드 Avant-garde

41 아겔다마-**박상륭** Akeldama-**Park Sang-ryoong**
42 내 영혼의 우물-**최인석** A Well in My Soul-**Choi In-seok**
43 당신에 대해서-**이인성** On You-**Yi In-seong**
44 회색 時-**배수아** Time In Gray-**Bae Su-ah**
45 브라운 부인-**정영문** Mrs. Brown-**Jung Young-moon**

바이링궐 에디션 한국 대표 소설 set 4

디아스포라 Diaspora

46 속옷-**김남일** Underwear-**Kim Nam-il**
47 상하이에 두고 온 사람들-**공선옥** People I Left in Shanghai-**Gong Sun-ok**
48 모두에게 복된 새해-**김연수** Happy New Year to Everyone-**Kim Yeon-su**
49 코끼리-**김재영** The Elephant-**Kim Jae-young**
50 먼지별-**이경** Dust Star-**Lee Kyung**

가족 Family

51 혜자의 눈꽃-**천승세** Hye-ja's Snow-Flowers-**Chun Seung-sei**
52 아베의 가족-**전상국** Ahbe's Family-**Jeon Sang-guk**
53 문 앞에서-**이동하** Outside the Door-**Lee Dong-ha**
54 그리고, 축제-**이혜경** And Then the Festival-**Lee Hye-kyung**
55 봄밤-**권여선** Spring Night-**Kwon Yeo-sun**

유머 Humor

56 오늘의 운세-**한창훈** Today's Fortune-**Han Chang-hoon**
57 새-**전성태** Bird-**Jeon Sung-tae**
58 밀수록 다시 가까워지는-**이기호** So Far, and Yet So Near-**Lee Ki-ho**
59 유리방패-**김중혁** The Glass Shield-**Kim Jung-hyuk**
60 전당포를 찾아서-**김종광** The Pawnshop Chase-**Kim Chong-kwang**

바이링궐 에디션 한국 대표 소설 set 5

관계 Relationship

61 도둑견습 – **김주영** Robbery Training-**Kim Joo-young**
62 사랑하라, 희망 없이 – **윤영수** Love, Hopelessly-**Yun Young-su**
63 봄날 오후, 과부 셋 – **정지아** Spring Afternoon, Three Widows-**Jeong Ji-a**
64 유턴 지점에 보물지도를 묻다 - **윤성희** Burying a Treasure Map at the U-turn-**Yoon Sung-hee**
65 쁘이거나 쯔이거나 - **백가흠** Puy, Thuy, Whatever-**Paik Ga-huim**

일상의 발견 Discovering Everyday Life

66 나는 음식이다 – **오수연** I Am Food-**Oh Soo-yeon**
67 트럭 – **강영숙** Truck-**Kang Young-sook**
68 통조림 공장 - **편혜영** The Canning Factory-**Pyun Hye-young**
69 꽃 – **부희령** Flowers-**Pu Hee-ryoung**
70 피의일요일 – **윤이형** BloodySunday-**Yun I-hyeong**

금기와 욕망 Taboo and Desire

71 북소리 - **송영** Drumbeat-**Song Yong**
72 발칸의 장미를 내게 주었네 - **정미경** He Gave Me Roses of the Balkans-**Jung Mi-kyung**
73 아무도 돌아오지 않는 밤 - **김숨** The Night Nobody Returns Home-**Kim Soom**
74 젓가락여자 - **천운영** Chopstick Woman-**Cheon Un-yeong**
75 아직 일어나지 않은 일 - **김미월** What Has Yet to Happen-**Kim Mi-wol**

바이링궐 에디션 한국 대표 소설 set 6

운명 Fate

76 언니를 놓치다 - **이경자** Losing a Sister-**Lee Kyung-ja**
77 아들 - **윤정모** Father and Son-**Yoon Jung-mo**
78 명두 - **구효서** Relics-**Ku Hyo-seo**
79 모독 - **조세희** Insult-**Cho Se-hui**
80 화요일의 강 - **손홍규** Tuesday River-**Son Hong-gyu**

미의 사제들 Aesthetic Priests

81 고수 - **이외수** Grand Master-**Lee Oisoo**
82 말을 찾아서 - **이순원** Looking for a Horse-**Lee Soon-won**
83 상춘곡 - **윤대녕** Song of Everlasting Spring-**Youn Dae-nyeong**
84 삭매와 자미 - **김별아** Sakmae and Jami-**Kim Byeol-ah**
85 저만치 혼자서 - **김훈** Alone Over There-**Kim Hoon**

식민지의 벌거벗은 자들 The Naked in the Colony

86 감자 - **김동인** Potatoes-**Kim Tong-in**
87 운수 좋은 날 - **현진건** A Lucky Day-**Hyŏn Chin'gŏn**
88 탈출기 - **최서해** Escape-**Ch'oe So-hae**
89 과도기 - **한설야** Transition-**Han Seol-ya**
90 지하촌 - **강경애** The Underground Village-**Kang Kyŏng-ae**

바이링궐 에디션 한국 대표 소설 set 7

백치가 된 식민지 지식인 Colonial Intellectuals Turned "Idiots"

91 날개 - **이상** Wings-**Yi Sang**
92 김 강사와 T 교수 - **유진오** Lecturer Kim and Professor T-**Chin-O Yu**
93 소설가 구보씨의 일일 - **박태원** A Day in the Life of Kubo the Novelist-**Pak Taewon**
94 비 오는 길 - **최명익** Walking in the Rain-**Ch'oe Myŏngik**
95 빛 속에 - **김사량** Into the Light-**Kim Sa-ryang**

한국의 잃어버린 얼굴 Traditional Korea's Lost Faces

96 봄·봄 – **김유정** Spring, Spring-**Kim Yu-jeong**
97 벙어리 삼룡이 – **나도향** Samnyong the Mute-**Na Tohyang**
98 달밤 – **이태준** An Idiot's Delight-**Yi T'ae-jun**
99 사랑손님과 어머니 – **주요섭** Mama and the Boarder-**Chu Yo-sup**
100 갯마을 – **오영수** Seaside Village-**Oh Yeongsu**

해방 전후(前後) Before and After Liberation

101 소망 – **채만식** Juvesenility-**Ch'ae Man-Sik**
102 두 파산 – **염상섭** Two Bankruptcies-**Yom Sang-Seop**
103 풀잎 – **이효석** Leaves of Grass-**Lee Hyo-seok**
104 맥 – **김남천** Barley-**Kim Namch'on**
105 꺼삐딴 리 – **전광용** Kapitan Ri-**Chŏn Kwangyong**

전후(戰後) Korea After the Korean War

106 소나기 – **황순원** The Cloudburst-**Hwang Sun-Won**
107 등신불 – **김동리** Tŭngsin-bul-**Kim Tong-ni**
108 요한 시집 – **장용학** The Poetry of John-**Chang Yong-hak**
109 비 오는 날 – **손창섭** Rainy Days-**Son Chang-sop**
110 오발탄 – **이범선** A Stray Bullet-**Lee Beomseon**